The Low-Cholesterol Diet Guide

Eat Well, Live Well

WELCOME

Welcome to the Low-Cholesterol Diet Guide: Eat Well, Live Well! I'm Wanda Walton, and I'm thrilled to share a heart-healthy approach to eating that's both delicious and effective. Whether you want to lower your cholesterol, improve your heart health, or adopt a more balanced lifestyle, this guide will help you achieve your goals.

My journey began with a deep passion for nutrition and a commitment to making healthier choices accessible to everyone. Through careful research and practical experience, I've created a guide filled with simple tips, structured meal plans, and nourishing and flavorful recipes.

Let's embark on this journey to better health together. Here's to making small changes that lead to a healthier, happier you!

Wanda Walton is a passionate advocate for heart health and nutrition. She is making her debut with The Low-Cholesterol Diet Guide: Eat Well, Live Well. With years of personal research and a deep commitment to promoting wellness, Wanda has crafted a comprehensive guide that bridges scientific knowledge and everyday practicality.

In her first book, Wanda provides readers with actionable strategies to lower cholesterol and improve heart health through simple yet effective dietary changes. This guide offers a clear roadmap to a healthier lifestyle, with expert tips, structured meal plans, and over 100 delicious recipes.

Wanda's approachable style and dedication to making wellness achievable for all make her debut an invaluable resource for anyone seeking lasting improvements to their health and well-being.

MEET WITH WANDA WALTON

01. WHAT IS THE CARNIVORE DIET?..........5

02. KEY DIETARY PRINCIPLES..........9

03. LUNCH..........36

04. DINNER..........62

05. DESSERTS..........89

06. MEAL PLANS AND DAILY MENUS..........115

07. THE SCIENCE OF CHOLESTEROL..........118

CHAPTER 1
KEY DIETARY PRINCIPLES

Strong hearts and healthy lives start with the right choices on your plate.

The Foundation of Heart-Healthy Eating

Strong hearts and healthy lives start with the right choices on your plate. Understanding what to eat—and what to avoid—is the first step toward lowering cholesterol and supporting overall health.

Focus on Whole Foods: Incorporate fruits, vegetables, whole grains, and legumes into every meal. These foods are rich in fiber, antioxidants, and nutrients that help reduce LDL ("bad") cholesterol and boost HDL ("good") cholesterol.

Example: Replace white bread with whole-grain options and sugary snacks with fresh fruit.

Choose Healthy Fats: Swap saturated fats (like butter and red meat) for unsaturated fats in olive oil, avocados, and nuts. Omega-3 fatty acids from fatty fish, such as salmon and mackerel, are particularly beneficial for heart health.

Limit Added Sugars and Refined Carbohydrates: High sugar intake can raise triglycerides and contribute to weight gain. Opt for whole grains instead of refined ones like white rice or pasta.

Practical Tips for Everyday Success

Adopting heart-healthy dietary principles can be simple and sustainable with these tips:

1. Read Labels: Look for hidden sugars, trans fats, and high sodium. Stick to products with minimal ingredients.
2. Cook at Home: Prepare meals by grilling, steaming, or baking instead of frying. Use herbs and spices instead of salt for flavour.
3. Plan Your Meals: Create a weekly meal plan that includes a variety of foods. This helps prevent unhealthy choices when you're short on time.
4. Practice Moderation: Enjoy your favourite treats occasionally but in small portions. Balance is critical to a sustainable diet.

Closing Thought:

"Every bite you take is a step toward better health. Let your plate reflect your care to your heart and body."

Foods to Include and Avoid

Creating a heart-healthy plate means knowing what to include and what to skip.

Foods to Include:

- Fruits and Vegetables: Fill half your plate with colourful options like berries, spinach, and broccoli. They're rich in soluble fibre and antioxidants.
- Whole Grains: Oats, quinoa, and barley help reduce cholesterol absorption into the bloodstream.
- Healthy Fats: Olive oil, nuts, seeds, and fatty fish support heart health and increase HDL levels.
- Legumes: Beans, lentils, and chickpeas are high in protein and fibre, making them great substitutes for meat.

Foods to Avoid:

- Saturated Fats: Found in full-fat dairy, butter, and red meat. Replace these with lean protein sources.
- Trans Fats: Avoid processed foods, baked goods, and fried items containing partially hydrogenated oils.
- Refined Carbohydrates: Limit white bread, sugary snacks, and drinks. Choose whole-grain alternatives.
- High-Sodium Foods: Processed and canned items can lead to high blood pressure, so choose low-sodium options.

CHAPTER 2
BREAKFAST

Nothing satisfies like a nourishing start to your day.

Berry Oatmeal

METHOD

- In a medium saucepan, bring the almond milk to a gentle boil.
- Add the rolled oats, reduce heat to a simmer, and cook for 5-7 minutes, stirring occasionally, until tender.
- Remove from heat and let it sit for a minute to thicken.
- Stir in the honey and mix well.
- Pour the oatmeal into a bowl, top with mixed berries, and sprinkle chia seeds.
- Serve warm and enjoy your heart-healthy breakfast!

INGREDIENT

1 cup rolled oats

2 cups almond milk

1 cup mixed berries (blueberries, raspberries, strawberries)

1 tbsp honey

1 tbsp chia seeds

NOTES

Feel free to swap almond milk with any plant-based or low-fat milk of your choice.

Avocado Toast with Tomato

METHOD

- Toast the whole grain bread until golden brown.
- While the bread is toasting, cut the avocado in half, remove the pit, and scoop the flesh into a bowl.
- Mash the avocado with a fork until smooth.
- Add the lemon juice and mix well.
- Spread the mashed avocado evenly over the toasted bread.
- Top each slice with cherry tomato slices.
- Sprinkle pepper over the tomatoes to taste.
- Serve immediately and enjoy this nutritious start to your day.

INGREDIENT

2 slices whole grain bread

1 ripe avocado

5 cherry tomatoes, sliced

1 tsp lemon juice

Pepper to taste

Greek Yogurt Parfait

METHOD

- In a tall glass or bowl, add a layer of Greek yoghurt (about half of the yoghurt).
- Add a layer of granola (about half) to the yoghurt.
- Add a layer of mixed berries (about half of the berries) on top of the granola.
- Repeat the layers with the remaining yoghurt, granola, and berries.
- Drizzle the honey over the top layer of berries.
- Serve immediately or refrigerate until ready to eat.

INGREDIENT

1 cup Greek yogurt
1/2 cup granola
1/2 cup mixed berries (blueberries, raspberries, strawberries)
1 tbsp honey

Veggie Omelette

INGREDIENT

4 egg whites

1 cup spinach, chopped

1/2 cup mushrooms, sliced

1/2 cup bell peppers, diced

1/4 cup onion, diced

1 tsp olive oil

METHOD

- Heat the olive oil in a non-stick skillet over medium heat.
- Add the diced onion and sauté for 2-3 minutes until translucent.
- Add the mushrooms, bell peppers, and spinach to the skillet. Cook for another 3-4 minutes until the vegetables are tender.
- Pour the egg whites over the vegetables in the skillet.
- Allow the egg whites to cook undisturbed for a few minutes until they start to set around the edges.
- Using a spatula, gently lift the edges of the omelette and tilt the skillet to let any uncooked egg whites flow to the edges.
- Once the egg whites are fully set, fold the omelette in half.
- Cook for another minute, then slide the omelette onto a plate.
- Serve hot and enjoy a protein-packed breakfast.

Banana Nut Smoothie

INGREDIENT

1 banana
1 cup almond milk
1 cup spinach
1 tbsp almond butter
1 tbsp flax seeds

METHOD

- Peel the banana and break it into chunks.
- Place the banana chunks, almond milk, spinach, almond butter, and flax seeds in a blender.
- Blend on high speed until smooth and creamy.
- Pour the smoothie into a glass.
- Serve immediately and enjoy this nutritious drink.

Chia Pudding

METHOD

- In a medium bowl, combine the chia seeds, almond milk, vanilla extract, and maple syrup.
- Stir well to mix all the ingredients.
- Cover the bowl and refrigerate overnight or for at least 4 hours.
- Stir the chia pudding once more before serving.
- Top with fresh berries.
- Serve chilled and enjoy a fibre-rich breakfast.

INGREDIENT

1/4 cup chia seeds
1 cup almond milk
1 tsp vanilla extract
1 tbsp maple syrup
1/2 cup berries (blueberries, raspberries, strawberries)

NOTES

Make the pudding the night before and let it sit in the fridge for at least 4 hours, preferably overnight, for the best consistency.

Whole Grain Pancakes

INGREDIENT

1 cup whole wheat flour

1 tsp baking powder

1 cup almond milk

2 egg whites

1/2 cup blueberries

METHOD

- In a large mixing bowl, combine the whole wheat flour and baking powder.
- In a separate bowl, whisk together the almond milk and egg whites.
- Pour the wet ingredients into the dry ingredients and stir until combined.
- Gently fold in the blueberries.
- Heat a non-stick skillet over medium heat and lightly coat with cooking spray.
- Pour 1/4 cup of batter onto the skillet for each pancake.
- Cook until bubbles form on the surface, then flip and cook until golden brown on the other side.
- Serve warm with additional blueberries or a drizzle of honey.

Apple Cinnamon Overnight Oats

METHOD

- In a mason jar or airtight container, combine the rolled oats, almond milk, diced apple, cinnamon, and honey.
- Stir well to mix all the ingredients.
- Cover and refrigerate overnight or for at least 4 hours.
- In the morning, give the oats a good stir.
- Serve cold or warm it up, and enjoy a nutritious start to your day.

INGREDIENT

1 cup rolled oats
1 cup almond milk
1 apple, diced
1 tsp cinnamon
1 tbsp honey

Spinach and Feta Breakfast Wrap

INGREDIENT

1 whole-grain tortilla
4 egg whites
1 cup spinach, chopped
1/4 cup feta cheese, crumbled
2 tbsp salsa

METHOD

- In a non-stick skillet, cook the spinach over medium heat until wilted.
- Add the egg whites to the skillet and scramble with the spinach until fully cooked.
- Lay the whole-grain tortilla on a flat surface.
- Spoon the spinach and egg mixture onto the centre of the tortilla.
- Sprinkle the feta cheese over the top.
- Add a spoonful of salsa.
- Roll up the tortilla, folding in the sides to enclose the filling.
- Serve immediately and enjoy a portable, protein-rich breakfast.

Sweet Potato and Black Bean Hash

INGREDIENT

1 sweet potato, peeled and diced
1 cup black beans, drained and rinsed
1 red bell pepper, diced
1/2 cup onion, diced
1 tsp olive oil
1 tsp cumin

METHOD

- Heat the olive oil in a large skillet over medium heat.
- Add the diced onion and cook for 2-3 minutes until translucent.
- Add the sweet potato to the skillet and cook for 10-12 minutes, stirring occasionally, until tender.
- Add the red bell pepper and cook for 3-4 minutes.
- Stir in the black beans and cumin, and cook for 2-3 minutes until heated.
- Season with salt and pepper to taste.
- Serve hot and enjoy a flavorful, filling breakfast.

Quinoa Breakfast Bowl

INGREDIENT

1 cup cooked quinoa

1 cup almond milk

1/2 cup strawberries, sliced

1/4 cup almonds, chopped

1 tbsp honey

NOTES

Add a poached egg, a dollop of Greek yogurt, or a sprinkle of nuts for extra protein.

METHOD

- In a medium saucepan, warm the cooked quinoa and almond milk over medium heat until heated.
- Transfer to a bowl and top with sliced strawberries, chopped almonds, and a drizzle of honey.
- Serve immediately and enjoy a nutritious breakfast.

Tomato and Basil Frittata

INGREDIENTS

4 egg whites
1 cup cherry tomatoes, halved
1/4 cup fresh basil, chopped
1 cup spinach
1 tsp olive oil

METHOD

- Preheat oven to 350°F (175°C).
- In an oven-safe skillet, heat olive oil over medium heat.
- Add cherry tomatoes, basil, and spinach; cook until spinach is wilted.
- Pour egg whites over the vegetables.
- Transfer skillet to the oven and bake for 15-20 minutes, or until egg whites are set.
- Serve warm.

Pumpkin Spice Overnight Oats

INGREDIENT
1 cup rolled oats
1 cup almond milk
1/2 cup pumpkin puree
1 tsp cinnamon
1/4 tsp nutmeg

METHOD

- In a jar, mix rolled oats, almond milk, pumpkin puree, cinnamon, and nutmeg.
- Stir well, cover, and refrigerate overnight.
- In the morning, stir again and enjoy cold or heat.

NOTES

Use honey, maple syrup, or a sugar substitute like stevia to match your sweetness preference.

Egg White and Veggie Muffins

METHOD

- Preheat oven to 350°F (175°C).
- In a bowl, whisk egg whites until slightly frothy.
- Add chopped spinach, bell peppers, onions, and mushrooms.
- Pour mixture into a greased muffin tin.
- Bake for 20-25 minutes or until egg whites are set.
- Serve warm or store for later.

INGREDIENT

8 egg whites
1 cup spinach, chopped
1/2 cup bell peppers, diced
1/4 cup onions, diced
1/2 cup mushrooms, diced

Zucchini Bread Oatmeal

METHOD

- In a saucepan, combine rolled oats and almond milk.
- Bring to a boil, then reduce heat and simmer for 5-7 minutes, stirring occasionally.
- Stir in grated zucchini, walnuts, and cinnamon.
- Cook for another 2-3 minutes until thickened.

INGREDIENT

1 cup rolled oats
2 cups almond milk
1 cup grated zucchini
1/4 cup walnuts, chopped
1 tsp cinnamon

NOTES

Grate zucchini finely and squeeze out excess moisture with a paper towel or clean kitchen cloth to avoid watery oatmeal.

Buckwheat Pancakes

INGREDIENT

1 cup buckwheat flour
1 tsp baking powder
1 cup almond milk
2 egg whites
1/2 cup blueberries

NOTES

For a gluten-free version, ensure the buckwheat flour is certified gluten-free or mix with almond flour for a lighter texture.

METHOD

- In a mixing bowl, combine buckwheat flour and baking powder.
- In another bowl, whisk together almond milk and egg whites.
- Pour the wet ingredients into the dry ingredients and stir until combined.
- Gently fold in the blueberries.
- Heat a non-stick skillet over medium heat and lightly grease with cooking spray.
- Pour 1/4 cup of batter onto the skillet for each pancake.
- Cook until bubbles form on the surface, then flip and cook until golden brown on the other side.
- Serve warm with additional blueberries or a drizzle of honey.

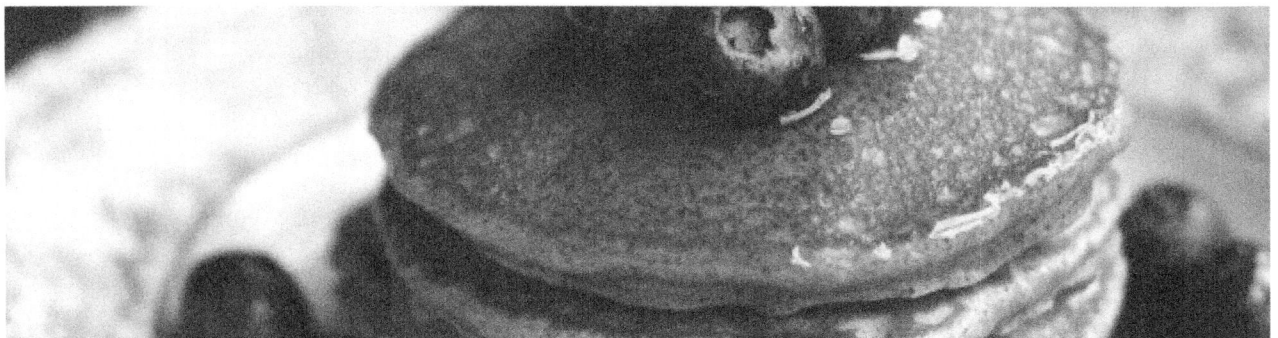

Tomato Avocado Smoothie

INGREDIENT

1 tomato, chopped

1 avocado, pitted and peeled

1/2 cup Greek yogurt

1 tbsp lemon juice

1 cup spinach

METHOD

- Place tomato, avocado, Greek yogurt, lemon juice, and spinach in a blender.
- Blend on high speed until smooth and creamy.
- Pour into a glass and serve immediately.

NOTES

Use ripe, flavorful tomatoes for the best taste. Cherry tomatoes work well for a slightly sweeter flavor.

Tropical Fruit Salad

INGREDIENT

1 cup pineapple, cubed
1 mango, cubed
1 kiwi, sliced

1 tbsp lime juice
1 tbsp fresh mint, chopped

NOTES

Use a mix of fresh tropical fruits such as pineapple, mango, kiwi, and papaya. Add berries or banana for variety.

METHOD

- In a large bowl, combine pineapple, mango, and kiwi.
- Drizzle lime juice over the fruit.
- Sprinkle with chopped mint and toss gently to combine.
- Serve immediately.

Kale and Mushroom Breakfast Bowl

METHOD

- Heat olive oil in a skillet over medium heat.
- Add kale and mushrooms and sauté until tender.
- Stir in cooked quinoa and cook until heated through.
- In a separate pan, cook egg whites until set.
- Serve the quinoa mixture, topped with cooked egg
- whites, in a bowl.

INGREDIENT

1 cup kale, chopped

1/2 cup mushrooms, sliced

1 cup cooked quinoa

1 tsp olive oil

4 egg whites

NOTES

Massage the kale with a drizzle of olive oil before cooking to make it tender and reduce bitterness.

Pumpkin Spice Overnight Oats

METHOD

- In a jar or container, combine rolled oats, almond milk, pumpkin puree, cinnamon, and nutmeg.
- Stir thoroughly to ensure all ingredients are well mixed.
- Cover the jar with a lid and refrigerate overnight, or for at least 6 hours.
- In the morning, stir the oats again and enjoy cold, or heat in the microwave or on the stove.

INGREDIENT

1 cup rolled oats

1 cup almond milk

1/2 cup pumpkin puree

1 tsp cinnamon

1/4 tsp nutmeg

NOTES

Garnish with chopped nuts, a sprinkle of granola, or a dollop of Greek yogurt.

Berry Almond Overnight Oats

METHOD

- In a mason jar or airtight container, combine rolled oats, almond milk, mixed berries, almond slices, and honey.
- Stir well, cover, and refrigerate overnight.
- In the morning, stir the oats and enjoy cold or warmed up

INGREDIENT

1 cup rolled oats
1 cup almond milk
1/2 cup mixed berries
1/4 cup almond slices
1 tbsp honey

NOTES

Use almond milk for a nutty flavor, or substitute with soy, oat, or low-fat dairy milk.

Spinach and Tomato Omelette

INGREDIENT

4 egg whites
1 cup spinach, chopped
1 tsp olive oil

1/2 cup cherry tomatoes, halved
Pepper to taste

METHOD

- Heat olive oil in a non-stick skillet over medium heat.
- Add the spinach and cherry tomatoes and cook until the spinach is wilted and the tomatoes are slightly softened.
- Pour the egg whites over the vegetables in the skillet.
- Allow the egg whites to cook undisturbed for a few minutes until they start to set around the edges.
- Using a spatula, gently lift the edges of the omelette and tilt the skillet to let any uncooked egg whites flow to the edges.
- Once the egg whites are fully set, fold the omelette in half.
- Cook for another minute, then slide the omelette onto a plate.
- Sprinkle with pepper to taste.
- Serve immediately and enjoy a protein-packed breakfast.

Berry Nut Breakfast Bars

INGREDIENT

1 cup oats

1/2 cup mixed nuts, chopped

1/4 cup dried berries

1/4 cup honey

1/4 cup almond butter

METHOD

- Preheat oven to 350°F (175°C).
- In a mixing bowl, combine oats, mixed nuts, and dried berries.
- In a small saucepan, heat honey and almond butter over low heat until melted and smooth.
- Pour the honey-almond butter mixture over the oat mixture and stir until well combined.
- Press the mixture firmly into a greased or parchment-lined baking dish.
- Bake for 15-20 minutes or until the golden brown bars are set.
- Allow to cool completely before cutting into bars.
- Store in an airtight container for up to a week.

Sweet Potato and Avocado Toast

METHOD

- Toast sweet potato slices in a toaster or oven until tender and slightly crispy.
- In a bowl, mash avocado with lime juice.
- Spread mashed avocado on the toasted sweet potato slices.
- Sprinkle with chilli flakes.
- Serve immediately.

NOTES

Use ripe avocado for easy spreading and a creamy texture. Add a squeeze of lemon or lime to prevent browning.

INGREDIENT

2 slices sweet potato, toasted

1 avocado, mashed

1 tsp lime juice

1/4 tsp chilli flakes

Egg White and Spinach Breakfast Sandwich

METHOD

- Toast the whole-grain English muffin.
- In a skillet, cook spinach over medium heat until wilted.
- Add egg whites to the skillet and scramble with the spinach
- until fully cooked.
- Assemble the sandwich with the egg white and spinach mixture and tomato slices.
- Serve immediately.

INGREDIENT

1 whole-grain English muffin

4 egg whites

1 cup spinach

2 tomato slices

NOTES

Use whole-grain bread or an English muffin for added fiber and a heart-healthy option.

Fuel your heart with the right foods; everything else will follow: health, vitality, and a life full of energy.

CHAPTER 3
LUNCH

Grilled Chicken Salad

METHOD

- In a large bowl, combine mixed greens, cherry tomatoes, red onion, and cucumbers.
- Top with grilled chicken slices.
- Drizzle with balsamic vinaigrette.
- Toss gently and serve immediately.

NOTES

Sprinkle with toasted nuts or seeds, such as almonds or sunflower seeds, for added texture and nutrition.

INGREDIENT

1 chicken breast, grilled and sliced

4 cups mixed greens

1/2 cup cherry tomatoes, halved

1/4 cup red onion, thinly sliced

1/4 cup cucumbers, sliced

2 tbsp balsamic vinaigrette

Lentil Soup

INGREDIENT

1 cup lentils, rinsed
1 onion, chopped
2 carrots, chopped
2 celery stalks, chopped
4 cups vegetable broth
1 tsp thyme
1 bay leaf

NOTES

Use green or brown lentils for a hearty texture. Red lentils cook faster but result in a creamier consistency.

METHOD

- In a large pot, sauté onion, carrots, and celery until soft.
- Add lentils, vegetable broth, thyme, and bay leaf.
- Bring to a boil, then reduce heat and simmer for 25-30 minutes.
- Remove bay leaf and serve hot.

Spinach and Mushroom Quiche

INGREDIENT

1 whole grain pie crust

4 egg whites

1 cup spinach, chopped

1/2 cup mushrooms, sliced

1/2 cup low-fat milk

1/4 cup feta cheese

NOTES

Use a whole-grain crust for added fiber, or go crustless for a lower-carb, lighter option.

METHOD

- Preheat oven to 350°F (175°C).
- In a bowl, whisk egg whites and milk.
- Add spinach, mushrooms, and feta cheese.
- Pour mixture into pie crust.
- Bake for 30-35 minutes until set.
- Serve warm.

Chickpea Salad Sandwich

METHOD

- In a bowl, mix mashed chickpeas, celery, red onion, Greek yoghurt, and lemon juice.
- Spread chickpea mixture on one slice of bread.
- Top with the other slice of bread.
- Serve immediately.

NOTES

Use canned chickpeas for convenience. Rinse and drain them thoroughly to reduce sodium.

INGREDIENT

1 cup chickpeas, mashed
1/4 cup diced celery
1/4 cup diced red onion
2 tbsp Greek yogurt
1 tbsp lemon juice
2 slices whole grain bread

Grilled Vegetable Wrap

INGREDIENT

1 whole-grain tortilla

1/2 cup grilled zucchini, sliced

1/2 cup grilled bell peppers, sliced

1/4 cup hummus

1/4 cup arugula

METHOD

- Spread hummus on the tortilla.
- Layer grilled zucchini, bell peppers, and arugula.
- Roll up tightly and slice in half.
- Serve immediately.

NOTES

Grill zucchini, bell peppers, eggplant, or mushrooms for a smoky, savory flavor.

Salmon and Asparagus

METHOD

- Preheat oven to 400°F (200°C).
- Place salmon and asparagus on a baking sheet.
- Drizzle with olive oil and sprinkle with lemon zest, salt, and pepper.
- Bake for 12-15 minutes until salmon is cooked through.
- Serve immediately.

INGREDIENT

1 salmon fillet
1 bunch asparagus, trimmed
1 tbsp olive oil
1 tsp lemon zest
Salt and pepper to taste

Chicken and Avocado Salad

METHOD

- In a large bowl, combine mixed greens, chicken, avocado, cherry tomatoes, and red onion.
- Drizzle with olive oil and balsamic vinegar.
- Toss gently and serve immediately.

INGREDIENT

2 cups mixed greens

1 grilled chicken breast, sliced

1 avocado, diced

1/2 cup cherry tomatoes, halved

1/4 cup red onion, sliced

2 tbsp olive oil

1 tbsp balsamic vinegar

NOTES

Add a light olive oil and lemon dressing or a yogurt-based dressing for a tangy, heart-healthy option.

Quinoa and Roasted Veggie Bowl

INGREDIENT

1 cup cooked quinoa

1 cup roasted vegetables (e.g., zucchini, bell peppers, carrots)

1/4 cup chickpeas

1 tbsp tahini

1 tbsp lemon juice

METHOD

- In a bowl, combine cooked quinoa, roasted vegetables, and chickpeas.
- Drizzle with tahini and lemon juice.
- Toss gently and serve.

NOTES

Use a mix of roasted vegetables like sweet potatoes, zucchini, bell peppers, and broccoli for a variety of textures and nutrients.

Turkey and Spinach Salad

INGREDIENT

4 cups spinach leaves
1/2 cup cooked turkey breast, sliced
1/4 cup dried cranberries
1/4 cup walnuts, chopped
2 tbsp balsamic vinaigrette

METHOD

- In a large bowl, combine spinach, turkey, dried cranberries, and walnuts.
- Drizzle with balsamic vinaigrette.
- Toss gently and serve immediately.

NOTES

Use lean, cooked turkey breast slices or leftover roasted turkey for a heart-healthy protein option.

Black Bean and Corn Salad

INGREDIENTS

1 cup black beans, drained and rinsed

1 cup corn kernels

1/2 red bell pepper, diced

1/4 cup red onion, diced

2 tbsp lime juice

1 tbsp olive oil

METHOD

- In a large bowl, combine black beans, corn, red bell pepper, and red onion.
- Drizzle with lime juice and olive oil.
- Toss gently and serve.

NOTES

Add a handful of toasted almonds, sunflower seeds, or dried cranberries for extra flavor and nutrients.

Tuna and White Bean Salad

INGREDIENT

1 can tuna, drained
1 cup white beans, drained and rinsed
1/2 cup cherry tomatoes, halved
1/4 cup red onion, diced
2 tbsp olive oil
1 tbsp lemon juice

NOTES

Use canned white beans (such as cannellini or navy beans) for convenience. Rinse and drain them thoroughly to reduce sodium.

METHOD

- In a large bowl, combine tuna, white beans, cherry tomatoes, and red onion.
- Drizzle with olive oil and lemon juice.
- Toss gently and serve immediately.

Asian Chicken Salad

METHOD

- In a large bowl, combine cabbage, chicken, carrots,
- and almonds.
- Drizzle with sesame dressing.
- Toss gently and serve immediately.

INGREDIENT

2 cups shredded cabbage
1 cup cooked chicken breast, sliced
1/2 cup shredded carrots
1/4 cup sliced almonds
2 tbsp sesame dressing

Avocado and Shrimp Salad

INGREDIENT

1 cup cooked shrimp, peeled and deveined

1 avocado, diced

2 cups mixed greens

1/2 cup cherry tomatoes, halved

1/4 cup red onion, sliced

2 tbsp olive oil

1 tbsp lime juice

METHOD

- In a large bowl, combine shrimp, avocado, mixed greens, cherry tomatoes, and red onion.
- Drizzle with olive oil and lime juice.
- Toss gently and serve immediately.

NOTES

Use cooked shrimp for convenience or sauté fresh shrimp with olive oil, garlic, and a squeeze of lemon for added flavor.

Broccoli and Almond Soup

INGREDIENT

42 cups broccoli florets
1 onion, chopped
2 garlic cloves, minced

4 cups vegetable broth
1/4 cup sliced almonds
1 tsp olive oil

METHOD

- In a large pot, heat olive oil and sauté onion and garlic until soft.
- Add broccoli and vegetable broth, boil, reduce heat and simmer for 15 minutes.
- Blend soup until smooth.
- Stir in sliced almonds and serve hot.

Tofu Stir-Fry

METHOD

- In a large skillet, heat olive oil and add tofu. Cook until browned.
- Add broccoli, bell pepper, and carrot. Stir-fry for 5-7 minutes.
- Add soy sauce and cook for another 2 minutes.
- Sprinkle with sesame seeds and serve.

INGREDIENT

1 block firm tofu, cubed

1 cup broccoli florets

1 red bell pepper, sliced

1 carrot, julienned

2 tbsp low-sodium soy sauce

1 tbsp olive oil

1 tsp sesame seeds

NOTES

Include diced cucumber, cherry tomatoes, and red onion for a refreshing crunch.

Chickpea and Spinach Stew

METHOD

- In a large pot, heat olive oil and sauté onion and garlic until soft.
- Add chickpeas, spinach, vegetable broth, and cumin.
- Bring to a boil, reduce heat, and simmer for 15 minutes.
- Serve hot.

INGREDIENT

1 can chickpeas, drained and rinsed

2 cups spinach leaves

1 onion, chopped

2 garlic cloves, minced

4 cups vegetable broth

1 tsp cumin

1 tbsp olive oil

NOTES

Use canned chickpeas for convenience, but rinse and drain thoroughly to reduce sodium. For a fresher taste, cook dried chickpeas ahead of time.

Cauliflower Rice Bowl

METHOD

- In a large bowl, combine cauliflower rice, black beans, corn, tomatoes, and avocado.
- Drizzle with lime juice. Toss gently and serve.

INGREDIENT

2 cups cauliflower rice
1 cup black beans, drained and rinsed
1/2 cup corn kernels
1/4 cup diced tomatoes
1 avocado, diced
1 tbsp lime juice

Grilled Portobello Mushrooms

METHOD

- In a small bowl, mix balsamic vinegar, olive oil, and minced garlic.
- Brush the mixture onto both sides of the portobello mushrooms.
- Grill mushrooms over medium heat for 5-7 minutes on each side.

INGREDIENT

2 large portobello mushrooms, stems removed

1 tbsp balsamic vinegar

1 tbsp olive oil

1 garlic clove, minced

NOTES

Gently clean mushrooms with a damp cloth and remove the stems for a smooth grilling surface.

Moroccan Chickpea Stew

METHOD

- In a large pot, heat olive oil and sauté onion and garlic until soft.
- Add chickpeas, tomatoes, vegetable broth, cumin, and cinnamon.
- Bring to a boil, reduce heat, and simmer for 20 minutes.
- Serve hot.

INGREDIENT

1 can chickpeas, drained and rinsed
1 cup diced tomatoes
1 onion, chopped
2 garlic cloves, minced
4 cups vegetable broth
1 tsp cumin
1/2 tsp cinnamon
1 tbsp olive oil

NOTES

Use canned chickpeas for convenience, rinsed and drained to reduce sodium. Alternatively, cook dried chickpeas for a fresher flavor.

CHAPTER 4
DINNER

Baked Lemon Herb Salmon

METHOD
- Preheat oven to 375°F (190°C).
- Place salmon fillets on a baking sheet lined with parchment paper.
- Drizzle with olive oil and season with thyme, rosemary, salt, and pepper.
- Top with lemon slices.
- Bake for 15-20 minutes, until salmon is cooked through.
- Serve immediately.

INGREDIENT
2 salmon fillets
1 lemon, sliced
1 tbsp olive oil
1 tsp dried thyme
1 tsp dried rosemary
Salt and pepper to taste

NOTES
Use fresh or thawed salmon fillets with the skin on to retain moisture during baking.

Quinoa and Veggie Stir-Fry

INGREDIENT

1 cup cooked quinoa

1 cup broccoli florets

1 red bell pepper, sliced

1 carrot, julienned

1/2 cup snap peas

2 tbsp low-sodium soy sauce

1 tbsp olive oil

METHOD

- Heat olive oil in a large skillet over medium heat.
- Add broccoli, bell pepper, carrot, and snap peas.
- Stir-fry for 5-7 minutes.
- Add cooked quinoa and soy sauce.
- Stir until well combined and heated through.
- Serve immediately.

NOTES

Include a colorful mix of bell peppers, zucchini, carrots, broccoli, and snap peas for variety and nutrients.

Grilled Chicken with Avocado Salsa

METHOD

- Preheat grill to medium-high heat.
- Season chicken breasts with salt and pepper.
- Grill chicken for 6-7 minutes on each side until fully cooked.
- In a bowl, combine avocado, cherry tomatoes, red onion, lime juice, and olive oil.
- Top grilled chicken with avocado salsa.
- Serve immediately.

INGREDIENT

2 chicken breasts

1 avocado, diced

1/2 cup cherry tomatoes, halved

1/4 cup red onion, diced

1 tbsp lime juice

1 tbsp olive oil

Salt and pepper to taste

Spaghetti Squash with Marinara Sauce

INGREDIENT

1 spaghetti squash
2 cups marinara sauce
1/4 cup grated Parmesan cheese
1 tbsp olive oil
Salt and pepper to taste

NOTES

Use homemade or store-bought marinara, opting for low-sodium options to keep it heart-healthy.

METHOD

- Preheat oven to 400°F (200°C).
- Cut spaghetti squash in half lengthwise and remove seeds.
- Drizzle with olive oil and season with salt and pepper.
- Place cut side on a baking sheet and bake for 40 minutes.
- Scrape squash with a fork to create spaghetti-like strands.
- Heat marinara sauce in a saucepan.
- Serve squash topped with marinara sauce and
- Parmesan cheese.

Turkey Meatballs with Zucchini Noodles

INGREDIENT

21 lb ground turkey

1/4 cup breadcrumbs

1 egg

1 tsp garlic powder

1 tsp onion powder

2 zucchinis, spiralized

1 cup marinara sauce

METHOD

- Preheat oven to 375°F (190°C).
- In a bowl, mix ground turkey, breadcrumbs, egg, garlic powder, and onion powder.
- Form into meatballs and place on a baking sheet.
- Bake for 20-25 minutes, until cooked through.
- Heat marinara sauce in a saucepan.
- Serve meatballs over zucchini noodles, topped with marinara sauce.

Lentil and Vegetable Stew

METHOD

- In a large pot, sauté onion, carrots, and celery until soft.
- Add lentils, vegetable broth, thyme, and bay leaf.
- Bring to a boil, then reduce heat and simmer for 25-30 minutes.
- Remove bay leaf and serve hot.

INGREDIENT

1 cup lentils, rinsed

2 carrots, chopped

2 celery stalks, chopped

1 onion, chopped

4 cups vegetable broth

1 tsp thyme

1 bay leaf

NOTES

Use low-sodium vegetable or chicken broth for a flavorful, heart-healthy base.

Baked Cod with Asparagus

INGREDIENT

2 cod fillets

1 bunch asparagus, trimmed

1 lemon, sliced

1 tbsp olive oil

Salt and pepper to taste

METHOD

- Preheat oven to 375°F (190°C).
- Place cod fillets and asparagus on a baking sheet lined with parchment paper.
- Drizzle with olive oil and season with salt and pepper.
- Top with lemon slices.
- Bake for 15-20 minutes, until cod is cooked through.
- Serve immediately.

NOTES

A simple mix of olive oil, lemon juice, minced garlic, and fresh dill or parsley enhances the natural flavors of the cod.

Chickpea and Spinach Curry

METHOD

- In a large pot, heat olive oil and sauté onion and garlic until soft.
- Add chickpeas, spinach, coconut milk, and curry powder.
- Bring to a boil, reduce heat, and simmer for 15 minutes.
- Serve hot.

INGREDIENT

1 can chickpeas, drained and rinsed

2 cups spinach leaves

1 onion, chopped

2 garlic cloves, minced

1 can coconut milk

1 tbsp curry powder

1 tbsp olive oil

NOTES

Fresh spinach works best, but frozen spinach can be substituted. Thaw and drain it before adding to the curry.

Shrimp and Broccoli Stir-Fry

METHOD

- In a large skillet, heat olive oil over medium heat.
- Add garlic and cook until fragrant.
- Add shrimp and cook until pink and opaque.
- Remove shrimp and set aside.
- Add broccoli and bell pepper to the skillet and stir-fry for 5-7 minutes.
- Return shrimp to the skillet and add soy sauce.
- Stir until well combined and heated through.
- Serve immediately.

NOTES

Cut broccoli into bite-sized florets for even cooking. You can blanch them briefly before stir-frying for a tender-crisp texture.

INGREDIENT

1 lb shrimp, peeled and deveined
2 cups broccoli florets
1 red bell pepper, sliced
2 garlic cloves, minced
2 tbsp low-sodium soy sauce
1 tbsp olive oil

Cauliflower Fried Rice

INGREDIENT

2 cups cauliflower rice

1 cup peas and carrots

2 garlic cloves, minced

2 tbsp low-sodium soy sauce

1 tbsp olive oil

2 green onions, chopped

METHOD

- In a large skillet, heat olive oil over medium heat.
- Add garlic and cook until fragrant.
- Add peas and carrots and cook for 5 minutes.
- Add cauliflower rice and soy sauce.
- Cook for an additional 5 minutes, stirring frequently.
- Stir in green onions and serve immediately.

NOTES

Scramble an egg or two and mix it into the fried rice for added protein and authenticity.

Baked Eggplant Parmesan

INGREDIENT

1 large eggplant, sliced

1 cup marinara sauce

1/2 cup grated Parmesan cheese

1 cup whole wheat breadcrumbs

2 egg whites

NOTES

Pair with a side salad or whole-grain pasta for a complete meal.

METHOD

- Preheat oven to 375°F (190°C).
- Dip eggplant slices in egg whites, then coat with breadcrumbs.
- Place on a baking sheet lined with parchment paper.
- Bake for 20-25 minutes, until crispy.
- Spread marinara sauce on the bottom of a baking dish.
- Layer baked eggplant slices on top, then sprinkle with Parmesan cheese.
- Bake for an additional 10 minutes, until cheese is melted.
- Serve hot.

Grilled Tofu with Vegetables

INGREDIENTS

1 block of firm tofu, pressed and sliced

1 red bell pepper, sliced

1 zucchini, sliced

1 tbsp olive oil

1 tbsp soy sauce

1 tsp garlic powder

METHOD

- Preheat grill to medium-high heat.
- In a bowl, mix olive oil, soy sauce, and garlic powder.
- Brush tofu and vegetables with the mixture.
- Grill tofu and vegetables for 5-7 minutes on each side.
- Serve immediately.

NOTES

Use a mix of soy sauce, sesame oil, garlic, ginger, and a touch of honey or maple syrup. Let tofu marinate for at least 30 minutes for maximum flavor.

Stuffed Bell Peppers

NOTES

Choose large, firm bell peppers with even bottoms so they stand upright easily during baking.

INGREDIENT

4 bell peppers, tops cut off and seeds removed
1 cup cooked quinoa
1 cup black beans, drained and rinsed
1 cup corn kernels
1/2 cup diced tomatoes
1 tsp cumin
1/2 tsp paprika

METHOD

- Preheat oven to 375°F (190°C).
- In a large bowl, mix quinoa, black beans, corn, tomatoes, cumin, and paprika.
- Stuff each bell pepper with the quinoa mixture.
- Place peppers in a baking dish for 25-30 minutes.
- Serve warm.

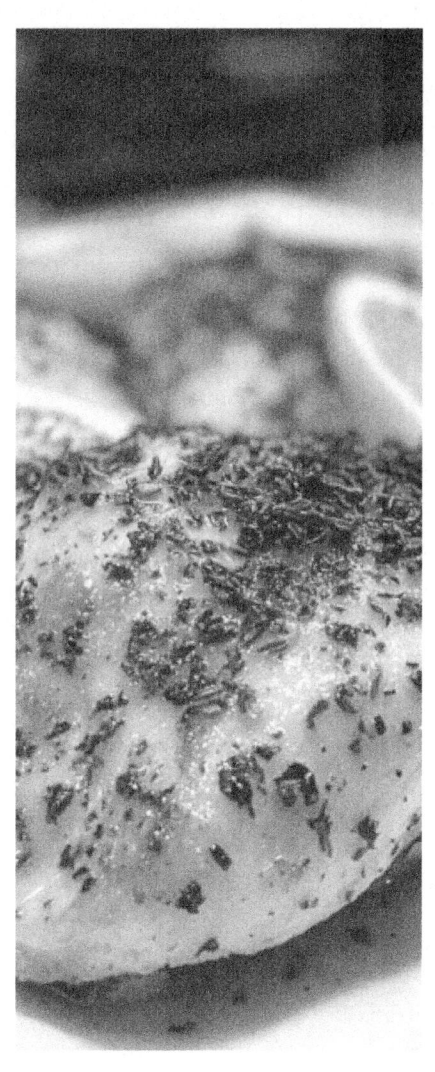

Lemon Herb Chicken

METHOD

- 1Preheat oven to 375°F (190°C).
- Place chicken breasts in a baking dish.
- Drizzle with olive oil and season with thyme, rosemary, salt, and pepper.
- Top with lemon slices.
- Bake for 25-30 minutes, until chicken is cooked through.
- Serve immediately.

NOTES

Add lemon slices and asparagus or green beans to the baking dish for a built-in side.

INGREDIENT

2 chicken breasts

1 lemon, sliced

1 tbsp olive oil

1 tsp dried thyme

1 tsp dried rosemary

Salt and pepper to taste

Zucchini Noodles with Pesto

METHOD

- Heat olive oil in a large skillet over medium heat.
- Add zucchini noodles and cook for 3-4 minutes until tender.
- Remove from heat and toss with basil pesto.
- Top with cherry tomatoes.
- Season with salt and pepper.

NOTES

Include cherry tomatoes, grilled chicken, or shrimp for a heartier meal.

INGREDIENT

2 zucchinis, spiralised

1/2 cup basil pesto

1/4 cup cherry tomatoes, halved

1 tbsp olive oil

Salt and pepper to taste

Baked Tilapia with Garlic and Lemon

INGREDIENT

2 tilapia fillets

2 garlic cloves, minced

1 lemon, sliced

1 tbsp olive oil

Salt and pepper to taste

METHOD

- Preheat oven to 375°F (190°C).
- Place tilapia fillets in a baking dish.
- Drizzle with olive oil and top with minced garlic and lemon slices.
- Season with salt and pepper.
- Bake for 15-20 minutes until fish is cooked through.

Sweet Potato and Black Bean Enchiladas

INGREDIENT

2 large sweet potatoes, peeled and diced

1 cup black beans, drained and rinsed

1/2 cup diced tomatoes

1/4 cup chopped cilantro

8 whole wheat tortillas

1 cup enchilada sauce

METHOD

- Preheat oven to 375°F (190°C).
- In a large pot, boil sweet potatoes until tender, then mash.
- In a bowl, mix mashed sweet potatoes, black beans, tomatoes, and cilantro.
- Fill each tortilla with the mixture and roll up.
- Place in a baking dish and top with enchilada sauce.
- Bake for 20-25 minutes.

NOTES

Use canned black beans for convenience, rinsed and drained to reduce sodium.

Chicken and Broccoli Stir-Fry

INGREDIENT

2 chicken breasts, sliced

2 cups broccoli florets

1 red bell pepper, sliced

2 garlic cloves, minced

2 tbsp low-sodium soy sauce

1 tbsp olive oil

METHOD

1. Preheat your oven to 350°F (175°C).

2. Pat the duck dry and season generously with salt and pepper.

3. Place the duck on a roasting rack in a baking pan. Roast for 1.5-2 hours until the skin is crispy.

4. Heat the beef bone broth in a small saucepan and stir in the orange juice (if using).

5. Let the duck rest for 10 minutes before carving. Serve with the pan juices.

Baked Chicken with Brussels Sprouts

METHOD

- Preheat your oven to 300°F (150°C).
- Heat the beef fat in a large Dutch oven over medium-high heat. Sear the chuck roast on all sides until browned, about 10 minutes.
- Add the beef bone broth, salt, black pepper, and garlic powder. Bring the mixture to a simmer.
- Cover the Dutch oven with a lid and transfer it to the oven. Cook for 3.5-4 hours until the meat is tender and falls apart easily.
- Let the pot roast rest for 10 minutes before slicing. Serve hot with the rich broth.

INGREDIENT

2 chicken breasts

2 cups Brussels sprouts, halved

1 tbsp olive oil

1 tbsp balsamic vinegar

Salt and pepper to taste

NOTES

Use skinless chicken thighs or breasts for a leaner, heart-healthy option.

Spaghetti with Lentil Bolognese

METHOD

- Heat olive oil in a large pot over medium heat.
- Add onion, garlic, and carrot, and cook until soft.
- Add lentils and diced tomatoes, and simmer for 15 minutes.
- Cook spaghetti according to package instructions.
- Serve lentil bolognese over spaghetti.

INGREDIENT

1 cup cooked lentils

1 can of diced tomatoes

1 onion, chopped

2 garlic cloves, minced

1 carrot, grated

1 tbsp olive oil

8 oz whole wheat spaghetti

NOTES

Use canned crushed tomatoes or a low-sodium marinara sauce to control salt levels.

Cauliflower and Chickpea Curry

METHOD

- Heat olive oil in a large pot over medium heat.
- Add onion and garlic, and cook until soft.
- Add cauliflower, chickpeas, coconut milk, and curry powder.
- Bring to a boil, reduce heat, and simmer for 20 minutes.

INGREDIENT

1 head cauliflower, chopped
1 can chickpeas, drained and rinsed
1 onion, chopped
2 garlic cloves, minced
1 can coconut milk
1 tbsp curry powder
1 tbsp olive oil

Grilled Salmon with Mango Salsa

INGREDIENT

2 salmon fillets
1 mango, diced
1/4 cup red onion, diced

1 tbsp lime juice
1 tbsp olive oil
Salt and pepper to taste

METHOD

- Preheat grill to medium-high heat.
- Season salmon fillets with salt and pepper.
- Grill salmon for 6-7 minutes on each side.
- In a bowl, combine mango, red onion, lime juice, and olive oil.
- Top grilled salmon with mango salsa.

NOTES

Lightly season salmon with olive oil, salt, pepper, and a squeeze of fresh lime juice for a simple, flavorful base.

Quinoa Stuffed Bell Peppers

INGREDIENT

4 bell peppers, tops cut off and seeds removed

1 cup cooked quinoa

1/2 cup black beans, drained and rinsed

1/2 cup corn kernels

1/4 cup diced tomatoes

1 tsp cumin

1/2 tsp paprika

METHOD

- 1Preheat oven to 375°F (190°C).
- In a large bowl, mix quinoa, black beans, corn, tomatoes, cumin, and paprika.
- Stuff each bell pepper with the quinoa mixture.
- Place peppers in a baking dish and bake for 25-30 minutes.

Fuel your heart with the right choices, and your whole body will thrive with strength and vitality.

CHAPTER 5
DESSERTS

A true feast is when wholesome, heart-healthy meals nourish both your body and soul.

Apple Cinnamon Yogurt Parfait

METHOD

- In a bowl, mix diced apple with cinnamon.
- Layer Greek yoghurt, apple mixture, and granola in a glass.
- Drizzle with honey.
- Serve immediately.

INGREDIENT

1 cup low-fat Greek yogurt
1 apple, diced
1 tsp cinnamon
1 tbsp honey
1/4 cup granola

NOTES

Use low-fat or Greek yogurt for a creamy, protein-rich base. Choose unsweetened yogurt to control sugar levels.

Banana Oat Cookies

INGREDIENT

2 ripe bananas, mashed
1 cup rolled oats
1/4 cup dark chocolate chips

NOTES

Enhance the cookies with mix-ins like dark chocolate chips, raisins, chopped nuts, or shredded coconut.

METHOD

- Preheat oven to 350°F (175°C).
- Mix mashed bananas and oats until combined.
- Fold in chocolate chips.
- Drop spoonfuls of the mixture onto a baking sheet.
- Bake for 15-20 minutes.
- Cool before serving.

Chia Seed Pudding

METHOD

- Mix chia seeds, almond milk, vanilla, and maple syrup in a bowl.
- Refrigerate overnight.
- Stir well before serving.
- Top with fresh berries.

NOTES

Stir the mixture thoroughly after the first 5-10 minutes of soaking to prevent clumps and ensure even distribution of seeds.

INGREDIENT

1/4 cup chia seeds
1 cup almond milk
1 tsp vanilla extract
1 tbsp maple syrup
1/2 cup fresh berries

Baked Apples with Cinnamon

INGREDIENT

4 apples, cored
1/4 cup raisins
1 tsp cinnamon
1 tbsp honey

METHOD

- Preheat oven to 350°F (175°C).
- Place cored apples in a baking dish.
- Fill each apple with raisins.
- Sprinkle with cinnamon and drizzle with honey.
- Bake for 30-35 minutes.
- Serve warm.

NOTES

Place apples in a baking dish and add a small amount of water or apple juice to the bottom to prevent burning and create a light sauce.

Pineapple Coconut Bars

INGREDIENT

1 cup crushed pineapple
1/2 cup shredded coconut
1/4 cup almond flour
1/4 cup honey

METHOD

- Preheat oven to 350°F (175°C). Line a baking dish with parchment paper for easy removal.
- Drain the crushed pineapple to remove excess liquid.
- Mix all ingredients in a bowl until well combined.
- Press the mixture evenly into the prepared baking dish, ensuring it's compact for even baking.
- Bake for 20-25 minutes, or until the edges are golden brown and the mixture is set.
- Let the bars cool completely in the dish before removing.
- Cut into bars and enjoy!

NOTES

Ensure the crushed pineapple is well-drained to prevent the mixture from becoming too wet. Excess moisture can affect the texture of the bars.

Baked Pears with Walnuts

INGREDIENT

4 pears, halved and cored

1/4 cup chopped walnuts

1 tbsp honey

1 tsp cinnamon

METHOD

- Preheat oven to 350°F (175°C). Lightly grease a baking dish.
- Wash pears, cut them in half lengthwise, and remove the core with a spoon or melon baller.
- Arrange the pear halves cut side up in the baking dish.
- Sprinkle chopped walnuts into the cored center of each pear.
- Drizzle honey over the pears and sprinkle with cinnamon.
- Bake for 25-30 minutes, or until the pears are tender and slightly golden.
- Let cool slightly before serving. Pair with yogurt or enjoy on its own.

Lemon Blueberry Muffins

INGREDIENT

1 cup whole wheat flour
1/2 cup Greek yogurt
1/4 cup honey
1/2 cup blueberries
1 lemon, zested and juiced

METHOD

- Preheat oven to 350°F (175°C).
- Mix flour, yogurt, honey, lemon zest, and juice in a bowl.
- Fold in blueberries.
- Spoon batter into muffin tins.
- Bake for 20-25 minutes.
- Cool before serving.

NOTES

Use fresh or frozen blueberries. If using frozen, do not thaw them to prevent the batter from becoming watery.

Strawberry Banana Ice Cream

METHOD

- Slice ripe bananas and hull strawberries; freeze for at least 4 hours.
- Add frozen bananas, strawberries, and almond milk to a blender or food processor.
- Blend until smooth, scraping down the sides as needed.
- Add almond milk 1 tablespoon at a time if the mixture is too thick.
- Taste and adjust sweetness with honey or maple syrup if desired.
- Scoop and serve immediately for soft-serve consistency.
- Transfer to a freezer-safe container and freeze for 1-2 hours for a firmer texture.
- Let sit at room temperature for 5 minutes before scooping.
- Top with fresh fruit, nuts, or shredded coconut.

INGREDIENT

2 ripe bananas, sliced and frozen
1 cup strawberries, hulled and frozen
1/4 cup almond milk

Coconut Macaroons

METHOD

- Preheat oven to 350°F (175°C). Line a baking sheet with parchment paper.
- In a bowl, mix shredded coconut, honey, egg whites, and vanilla extract until well combined.
- Use a tablespoon or cookie scoop to drop spoonfuls of the mixture onto the prepared baking sheet.
- Shape the mixture into small mounds with slightly flattened tops.
- Bake for 15-20 minutes, or until the edges are golden brown.
- Allow the macaroons to cool on the baking sheet for 5 minutes before transferring to a wire rack.
- Serve immediately or store in an airtight container for up to 5 days.

INGREDIENT

2 cups shredded coconut
1/4 cup honey
2 egg whites
1 tsp vanilla extract

Chocolate Avocado Brownies

INGREDIENT

2 ripe avocados, mashed

1/2 cup cocoa powder

1/2 cup honey

1/2 cup whole wheat flour

1/4 cup dark chocolate chips

METHOD

- Preheat oven to 350°F (175°C). Grease a baking dish or line it with parchment paper.
- In a mixing bowl, mash ripe avocados until smooth and creamy.
- Add cocoa powder, honey, whole wheat flour, and dark chocolate chips to the mashed avocados. Mix until well combined and the batter is smooth.
- Pour the batter into the prepared baking dish, spreading it evenly with a spatula.
- Bake for 25-30 minutes or until a toothpick inserted into the center comes clean.
- Let the brownies cool completely in the dish before cutting them into squares.
- Serve immediately or store in an airtight container in the fridge for up to 5 days.

Mixed Berry Crisp

INGREDIENT

1. 2 cups mixed berries
2. 1/2 cup rolled oats
3. 1/4 cup almond flour
4. 1/4 cup honey
5. 1/4 cup chopped almonds

NOTES

Use fresh or frozen mixed berries like blueberries, raspberries, and blackberries. If using frozen, thaw and drain excess liquid.

METHOD

- Preheat oven to 350°F (175°C).
- Place berries in a baking dish.
- Mix oats, almond flour, honey, and almonds in a bowl.
- Sprinkle mixture over berries.
- Bake for 20-25 minutes.
- Serve warm.

Apple Walnut Salad

INGREDIENTS

2 apples, diced

1/4 cup chopped walnuts

1/4 cup raisins

1 tbsp honey

1 tsp cinnamon

METHOD

- Wash and dice the apples into bite-sized pieces, leaving the skin on for added fiber.
- Combine the diced apples, chopped walnuts, and raisins in a mixing bowl.
- Drizzle honey over the mixture and sprinkle with cinnamon.
- Toss everything gently to ensure the apples and nuts are evenly coated.
- Serve immediately as a refreshing salad or snack.
- For a chilled option, refrigerate for 15 minutes before serving.
- Enjoy on its own or as a side dish for a heart-healthy meal.

Peach Yogurt Popsicles

NOTES

Opt for low-fat Greek yogurt or a dairy-free alternative to suit dietary preferences.

INGREDIENT

2 ripe peaches, peeled and sliced
1 cup Greek yogurt
1/4 cup honey

METHOD

- Peel and slice the ripe peaches, removing the pit.
- Add the peaches, Greek yoghurt, and honey to a blender or food processor.
- Blend the mixture until smooth and creamy.
- Pour the blended mixture evenly into popsicle moulds, tapping the moulds gently to remove air bubbles.
- Insert popsicle sticks into the moulds.
- Freeze for at least 4 hours or until completely solid.
- To serve, run the moulds under warm water for a few seconds to release the popsicles easily.

Raspberry Chia Pudding

INGREDIENT

1/4 cup chia seeds
1 cup almond milk
1/2 cup raspberries
1 tbsp honey

METHOD

- Combine chia seeds, almond milk, and honey in a mixing bowl.
- Stir thoroughly to ensure the chia seeds are evenly distributed.
- Cover the bowl and refrigerate for at least 4 hours, preferably overnight, to allow the chia seeds to absorb the liquid and form a pudding-like consistency.
- Stir the mixture again before serving to break up any clumps.
- Top with fresh raspberries just before serving.
- Optionally, garnish with a drizzle of honey or a few mint leaves for added flavor.
- Enjoy chilled as a breakfast, snack, or light dessert.

NOTES

Swap almond milk with coconut milk, oat milk, or dairy milk for a different flavor and texture.

Blueberry Lemon Bars

METHOD

- Preheat oven to 350°F (175°C). Line a baking dish with parchment paper for easy removal.
- Mix whole wheat flour, Greek yoghurt, honey, lemon zest, and lemon juice in a mixing bowl. Mix until smooth.
- Gently fold in the blueberries to avoid breaking them.
- Pour the batter evenly into the prepared baking dish, spreading it with a spatula.
- Bake for 20-25 minutes until the edges are golden and a toothpick inserted into the centre comes out clean.
- Allow the bars to cool completely in the baking dish before removing.
- Cut into bars and serve.

INGREDIENT

1 cup whole wheat flour
1/2 cup Greek yogurt
1/4 cup honey
1/2 cup blueberries
1 lemon, zested and juiced

NOTES

Swap almond milk with coconut milk, oat milk, or dairy milk for a different flavor and texture.

Banana Chia Pudding

INGREDIENT

1/4 cup chia seeds
1 cup almond milk
1 ripe banana, mashed
1 tsp vanilla extract

NOTES

Stir the mixture after 10-15 minutes of refrigeration to prevent clumping.

METHOD

- In a mixing bowl, combine chia seeds, almond milk, mashed banana, and vanilla extract.
- Stir thoroughly to ensure the chia seeds are evenly distributed and the banana is well incorporated.
- Cover the bowl and refrigerate for at least 4 hours, preferably overnight, to allow the chia seeds to absorb the liquid and thicken.
- Stir the pudding again before serving to break up any clumps.
- Serve chilled as a breakfast, snack, or dessert.
- Optionally, top with sliced banana, nuts, or a sprinkle of cinnamon for added flavor.

Chocolate Dipped Strawberries

INGREDIENT

1 cup dark chocolate chips
1 lb strawberries

NOTES

Sprinkle with sea salt, chopped nuts, or drizzle with contrasting melted chocolate for a decorative touch.

METHOD

- Wash and dry the strawberries thoroughly. Ensure they are completely dry to help the chocolate adhere properly.
- Melt the dark chocolate chips in a microwave-safe bowl, heating in 30-second intervals and stirring after each interval until smooth and fully melted.
- Hold each strawberry by the stem and dip it into the melted chocolate, coating it halfway or to your desired level.
- Place the dipped strawberries on a baking sheet lined with parchment paper to prevent sticking.
- Optional: Drizzle the remaining chocolate over the strawberries or sprinkle with chopped nuts, coconut flakes, or sprinkles for decoration.
- Refrigerate the strawberries for 15-20 minutes or until the chocolate is fully set.
- Serve chilled, and enjoy immediately.

Cinnamon Baked Peaches

INGREDIENT

14 peaches, halved and pitted
1/4 cup chopped pecans
1 tbsp honey
1 tsp cinnamon

NOTES

Substitute pecans with walnuts, almonds, or hazelnuts for a different flavor profile.

METHOD

- Preheat oven to 350°F (175°C). Lightly grease a baking dish or line it with parchment paper.
- Wash the peaches, cut them in half, and remove the pits.
- Arrange the peach halves cut side up in the prepared baking dish.
- Sprinkle chopped pecans into the hollow of each peach half.
- Drizzle honey evenly over the peaches, ensuring each half gets a light coating.
- Sprinkle cinnamon over the peaches for a warm, aromatic flavour.
- Bake in the oven for 20-25 minutes or until the peaches are tender and slightly caramelized.
- Serve warm, optionally topped with a dollop of Greek yoghurt or a scoop of vanilla yoghurt.

Coconut Chia Pudding

NOTES

Use full-fat coconut milk for a richer pudding or light coconut milk for a lower-calorie option.

INGREDIENT

1/4 cup chia seeds

1 cup coconut milk

1 tsp vanilla extract

1 tbsp maple syrup

METHOD

- Combine chia seeds, coconut milk, vanilla extract, and maple syrup in a mixing bowl.
- Stir thoroughly to ensure the chia seeds are evenly distributed and begin absorbing the liquid.
- Cover the bowl and refrigerate for at least 4 hours, preferably overnight, to allow the mixture to thicken.
- Before serving, stir the pudding again to break up any clumps and ensure a smooth consistency.
- Serve chilled as a breakfast, snack, or light dessert.
- Optionally, top with fresh fruit, shredded coconut, or chopped nuts for added flavour and texture.

Mango Raspberry Smoothie Bowl

METHOD

- Peel and cube the mango, and rinse the raspberries.
- Combine mango, raspberries, Greek yoghurt, and almond milk in a blender.
- Blend until smooth and creamy, scraping down the sides as needed.
- Pour the blended mixture into a bowl, spreading it evenly.
- Top with fresh raspberries, granola, or additional toppings of your choice.
- Serve immediately for the freshest taste and best texture.

INGREDIENT

1 mango, peeled and cubed
1/2 cup raspberries
1/2 cup Greek yogurt
1/4 cup almond milk

NOTES

Substitute almond milk with coconut milk or oat milk for a different flavor profile.

Baked Banana with Almond Butter

METHOD

- Preheat oven to 350°F (175°C). Line a baking sheet with parchment paper for easy cleanup.
- Slice the bananas lengthwise and arrange them cut side up on the prepared baking sheet.
- Drizzle almond butter evenly over the banana slices.
- Drizzle with honey and sprinkle with cinnamon for added sweetness and flavour.
- Bake in the oven for 10-12 minutes or until the bananas are warm and slightly softened.
- Serve warm as a quick snack or light dessert.

INGREDIENT

2 bananas, sliced lengthwise
2 tbsp almond butter
1 tbsp honey
1/4 tsp cinnamon

Orange Almond Cake

INGREDIENT

1 cup almond flour
1/2 cup Greek yogurt
1/4 cup honey

1 orange, zested and juiced
2 eggs

METHOD

- Preheat oven to 350°F (175°C). Grease a baking dish or line it with parchment paper.
- Combine almond flour, Greek yoghurt, honey, orange zest, and orange juice in a mixing bowl. Mix until well combined.
- Add eggs to the mixture and beat until the batter is smooth and creamy.
- Pour the batter into the prepared baking dish, spreading it evenly with a spatula.
- Bake for 25-30 minutes until the top is golden, and a toothpick inserted into the centre comes out clean.
- Allow the cake to cool completely in the dish before slicing.
- Serve as is or with a dollop of Greek yoghurt and a sprinkle of orange zest

Strawberry Chia Jam

INGREDIENT

2 cups strawberries, hulled and chopped

2 tbsp chia seeds

1 tbsp honey

NOTES

Replace honey with maple syrup, agave syrup, or a sugar-free sweetener, adjusting to taste.

METHOD

- In a saucepan, cook strawberries over medium heat until softened and juices are released, about 5-7 minutes.
- Mash the strawberries to your desired consistency.
- Stir in chia seeds and honey, and simmer for 5-10 minutes until thickened.
- Remove from heat, let cool, and transfer to a jar.
- Serve as a topping for yoghurt, toast, or pancakes.

Apple Walnut Crisp

METHOD

- Preheat oven to 350°F (175°C). Lightly grease a baking dish or line it with parchment paper.
- Arrange the apple slices evenly in the baking dish.
- Combine rolled oats, almond flour, chopped walnuts, honey, and cinnamon in a mixing bowl. Mix until crumbly.
- Sprinkle the oat mixture evenly over the apples.
- Bake for 20-25 minutes or until the topping is golden brown and the apples are tender.
- Serve warm, optionally topped with Greek yoghurt or a scoop of vanilla yoghurt.

INGREDIENT

4 apples, peeled and sliced
1/2 cup rolled oats
1/4 cup almond flour
1/4 cup chopped walnuts
1 tbsp honey
1 tsp cinnamon

NOTES

Replace honey with maple syrup or agave syrup for a different flavour.

Almond Butter Energy Bites

METHOD

- Combine rolled oats, almond butter, honey, and flax seeds in a mixing bowl. Stir until fully combined.
- Roll the mixture into bite-sized balls using your hands or a small scoop.
- Place the energy bites on a plate or baking sheet lined with parchment paper.
- Refrigerate for at least 30 minutes to firm up.
- Serve chilled, and enjoy.

INGREDIENT

1 cup rolled oats

1/2 cup almond butter

1/4 cup honey

1/4 cup flax seeds

NOTES

Use maple syrup or agave syrup instead of honey, if preferred.

CHAPTER 6
Meal Plans and Daily Menus

A balanced life begins with a well-planned, heart-healthy plate.

Meal planning is essential for maintaining a heart-healthy, low-cholesterol diet. It ensures balanced nutrition, reduces decision fatigue, and helps avoid unhealthy food choices. You can create delicious and effective menus that manage cholesterol by focusing on variety and preparation.

Key Principles of Meal Planning:

1. Balance Macronutrients: Each meal should include lean proteins, whole grains, and healthy fats.
2. Incorporate Fiber: Soluble fiber, found in oats, beans, and fruits, helps reduce LDL cholesterol.
3. Hydration Matters: Water aids digestion and prevents mistaking thirst for hunger.
4. Preparation is Key: Cooking in batches and organizing ingredients saves time and ensures adherence to the plan.
5. Portion Control: Eating appropriate portions helps manage calorie intake while supporting cholesterol management.
6. Snack Smart: Choose healthy snacks, such as nuts, seeds, and vegetables with hummus, to maintain energy levels.

Sample Meal Plan

Day 1:

- Breakfast:

Whole Grain Pancakes

- Lunch:

Lentil Soup

- Afternoon Snack:

Carrot sticks with hummus.

- Dinner:

Baked Cod with Asparagus

- Dessert (Optional):

Orange Almond Cake

Day 2:

- Breakfast:

Egg White and Veggie Muffins

- Lunch:

Mediterranean Couscous Salad

- Afternoon Snack:

Celery sticks with peanut butter.

- Dinner:

Shrimp and Broccoli Stir-Fry

- Dessert (Optional):

Banana Chia Pudding

Sample Meal Plan

Day 3:
- Breakfast:

Berry Oatmeal
- Lunch:

Spinach and Mushroom Quiche
- Afternoon Snack:

Apple Slices with Almond Butter
- Dinner:

Baked Chicken with Brussels Sprouts
- Dessert (Optional):

Mixed Berry Crisp

Day 4:
- Breakfast:

Greek Yogurt Parfait
- Lunch:

Grilled Vegetable Wrap
- Afternoon Snack:

Carrot and Cucumber Sticks with Hummus
- Dinner:

Chicken and Vegetable Kebabs
- Dessert (Optional):

Mango Raspberry Smoothie Bowl

Sample Meal Plan

Day 5:
- Breakfast:

Spinach and Feta Breakfast Wrap

- Lunch:

Tuna and White Bean Salad

- Afternoon Snack:

Frozen GrapesFrozen Grapes

- Dinner:

Baked Cod with Asparagus

- Dessert (Optional):

Chocolate Dipped Strawberries

Day 6:
- Breakfast:

Quinoa Breakfast Bowl

- Lunch:

Broccoli and Almond Soup

- Afternoon Snack:

Air-Popped Popcorn

- Dinner:

Grilled Tofu with Vegetables

- Dessert (Optional):

Cinnamon Baked Peaches

CHAPTER 7
The Science of Cholesterol

Understanding Good and Bad Cholesterol

Cholesterol is a waxy substance in your blood, essential for building cells and producing hormones. However, not all cholesterol is created equal. There are two main types:

- Low-density lipoprotein (LDL): Known as "bad" cholesterol, LDL can build up in the walls of your arteries, leading to blockages and increasing the risk of heart disease and stroke.
- High-density lipoprotein (HDL): Known as "good" cholesterol, HDL helps remove LDL from the arteries and transports it to the liver for elimination.

The balance between LDL and HDL is critical for maintaining heart health. Diet, physical activity, genetics, and lifestyle choices influence cholesterol levels. Foods high in saturated fats, trans fats, and added sugars increase LDL levels, while fiber-rich foods, healthy fats, and regular exercise can boost HDL.

Understanding and managing your cholesterol levels is key to reducing the risk of cardiovascular disease and supporting long-term well-being.

CHAPTER 8
EXERCISE AND
LIFESTYLE TIPS

Yoga for Stress and Cholesterol Management

Yoga combines gentle physical movement, breathing exercises, and meditation. Its benefits include:

- Reducing stress: Chronic stress can elevate cholesterol and blood pressure. Yoga helps calm the mind and lower cortisol levels.
- Improving circulation: Stretching and postures increase blood flow, supporting cardiovascular health.
- Enhancing mindfulness: A balanced mind-body connection encourages healthier lifestyle choices, like better eating habits and exercise consistency.
- Promoting flexibility: Yoga keeps the body agile, preventing injuries and supporting overall physical wellness.

Stress Management Techniques

Stress can lead to unhealthy habits, such as poor diet choices and inactivity, which raise cholesterol. Managing stress is key to heart health:

- Deep Breathing: Simple breathing exercises calm the nervous system and reduce anxiety.
- Meditation and Mindfulness: Even 10 minutes a day can improve mental clarity and lower stress.
- Sleep Hygiene: Quality sleep (7-8 hours) supports stress reduction and overall heart health.

CONCLUSION

Congratulations on this vital step toward a healthier heart and a more vibrant life! This journey taught you how to make thoughtful food choices, craft balanced meal plans, and prepare delicious recipes that support your goals. By focusing on heart-healthy ingredients and understanding the science behind cholesterol, you've set yourself up for long-term success.

This guide is more than a collection of recipes; it's a lifestyle roadmap. By incorporating fiber-rich foods, healthy fats, and nutrient-dense meals into your daily routine, you can reduce cholesterol levels, improve energy, and feel your best every day.

Remember, consistency is the foundation of sustainable health. Use this book's tips, meal plans, and practical advice to create habits that support your well-being. Don't hesitate to adjust recipes, explore new ingredients, or adapt the plans to suit your preferences and lifestyle.

As you move forward, celebrate each small victory and trust the process. Healthy living isn't about perfection—it's about progress. Every choice you make brings you closer to your goals.

Here's to a stronger, healthier, and happier you. May this guide inspire you to make choices that nurture your heart and body for years.

Happy Cooking and Healthy Eating!

THANK YOU

Thank you for choosing *The Low-Cholesterol Diet Guide: Eat Well, Live Well*. Your journey to healthier meals starts here, and I'm thrilled to support you.

As a special thank-you, I've prepared 5 exclusive bonus recipes to inspire your healthy cooking journey. Scan the QR code below, provide your email, and the recipes will be sent straight to your inbox.

You help me continue creating valuable resources for those seeking a healthier lifestyle. Thank you for participating in this journey toward better health and wellness.

With heartfelt gratitude,
Wanda Walton

RECIPE TESTING

RECIPE NAME	RATING	NOTE
_____	☆☆☆☆☆	_____
_____	☆☆☆☆☆	_____
_____	☆☆☆☆☆	_____
_____	☆☆☆☆☆	_____
_____	☆☆☆☆☆	_____
_____	☆☆☆☆☆	_____
_____	☆☆☆☆☆	_____
_____	☆☆☆☆☆	_____
_____	☆☆☆☆☆	_____
_____	☆☆☆☆☆	_____
_____	☆☆☆☆☆	_____
_____	☆☆☆☆☆	_____
_____	☆☆☆☆☆	_____
_____	☆☆☆☆☆	_____

MEAL PLANNER

	BREAKFAST	LUNCH	DINNER	DESSERT
MON				
TUE				
WEN				
THU				
FRI				
SAT				
SUN				

GROCERY LIST

VEGETABLES	MEAT & FISH	FRUITS
_____	_____	_____
_____	_____	_____
_____	_____	_____
_____	_____	_____
_____	_____	_____

CANS & JARS	BREADS & GRAINS	BAKERY & SEASONING
_____	_____	_____
_____	_____	_____
_____	_____	_____
_____	_____	_____
_____	_____	_____

DAIRY & DRINKS	FROZEN FOODS	HOUSEHOLD
_____	_____	_____
_____	_____	_____
_____	_____	_____
_____	_____	_____
_____	_____	_____

Printed in Great Britain
by Amazon